Solar System

KINGFISHER

Kingfisher Publications Plc
New Penderel House,
283–288 High Holborn,
London WC1V 7HZ
www.kingfisherpub.com

First published by Kingfisher Publications Plc 2004
4 6 8 10 9 7 5 3

3TR/0705/PROSP/RNB(RNB)/140MA/F

A CIP catalogue record for this book is available from the British Library.

ISBN–13: 978 0 7534 0922 0
ISBN–10: 0 7534 0922 4

Editor: Jennifer Schofield
Designer: Joanne Brown
Cover designer: Mike Buckley
Picture manager: Cee Weston-Baker
Picture researcher: Harriet Merry
Artwork archivists: Wendy Allison and Jennifer Lord
DTP manager: Nicky Studdart
Production controller: Oonagh Phelan
Indexer: Sheila Clewley

Printed in China

Acknowledgements
The publisher would like to thank the following for permission to reproduce their material. Every care has been
taken to trace copyright holders. However, if there have been unintentional omissions or failure to trace
copyright holders, we apologise and will, if informed, endeavour to make corrections in any future edition.
b = bottom, c = centre, l = left, t = top, r = right

Cover: Cassini probe: Science Photo Library (SPL); Earth's surface: SPL; 2–3 National Geographic; 4–5 NASA/Corbis;
6–7 NASA/SPL; 8bl Getty Images; 8–9 Getty Images; 10cl SPL; 10–11 NASA; 11b Corbis; 12–13 NASA/Corbis; 13tl Corbis;
13bl Mary Evans Picture Library; 16 Getty Images; 17t Getty Images; 18–19 Corbis; 18r NASA; 19t Getty Images;
19b Getty Images; 20–21 NASA; 21tr NASA; 21bl NASA; 22bl Galaxy; 22cr NASA/SPL; 23t Corbis; 23b NASA; 24c SPL;
24–25 NASA; 25b Kobal Collection; 26–27t NASA/SPL; 27cl NASA/SPL; 27br Corbis; 28–29 Corbis; 30c SPL; 30–31 Corbis;
31tr Corbis; 32–33 NASA/SPL; 33tr NASA/SPL; 37br NASA/SPL; 38bl The Art Archive; 38–39 Corbis; 39br Corbis;
40–41t Getty Images; 40–41b Galaxy Picture Library; 42–43 NASA/Corbis; 47br Alamy Images; 48br Corbis.

Commissioned artwork on pages 34–35 and 40–44 by Daniel Shutt; commissioned photography on pages 44–47 by Andy Crawford
Project-maker and photoshoot co-ordinator: Miranda Kennedy
Thank you to models Holly Hadaway and Sonnie Nash

Kingfisher Young Knowledge

Solar System

Dr Mike Goldsmith

Contents

Solar System

The Earth that we live on, the Sun and the Moon are all parts of the Solar System. It is called the Solar System because everything goes around the Sun and solar means 'of the Sun'.

Other worlds

There are nine planets in the Solar System and Earth is just one of them. Most of the planets also have moons going around them.

Sun

Mars

Earth

Venus

Mercury

Uranus

Pluto

Neptune

Saturn

Jupiter

Space rocks

The Sun, planets and
moons are not the only
things in the Solar System.
There are comets, asteroids,
meteoroids, dust and gases
too. Comets are like huge
dirty snowballs. Asteroids
are giant chunks of rock
and meteoroids are small
pieces of rock.

Round and round

All nine planets in the Solar System travel through space, going around the Sun. The time that it takes a planet to go around the Sun once is called a year.

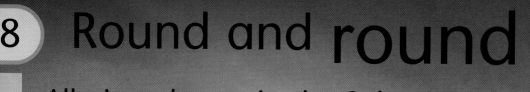

The pull of gravity

The force that pulls things towards each other is called gravity. If you throw a football into the air, it is gravity that pulls it down again. The Sun's gravity holds the planets in place. If there was no gravity, the Earth would fall to pieces and you would be thrown into space.

Sun

Earth

Around the Sun

Earth goes around the Sun in about 365 days. Planets closer to the Sun have shorter orbits, so they go around it quicker. Mercury's year is 88 days.

Day and night

Each planet also spins around, causing it to have day and night. On other planets, these are not the same length as Earth's. The days on Venus are 243 times longer than ours!

orbit – *the path of one object around another in space*

Fiery star

The Sun is the only star in the Solar System. It is so big, Earth could fit into it a million times! The Sun is also very hot – much hotter than an oven.

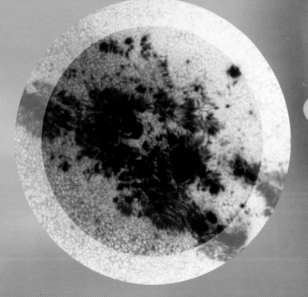

Spotty Sun
The surface of the Sun is constantly moving. Sometimes, dark, cool spots form on the Sun's surface. These spots are called sunspots.

star – *an enormous, glowing ball of very hot gas*

Great balls of fire

Prominences are giant masses of gas thrown off by the Sun. They look just like the leaping flames of a fire.

Warning! Hot Sun

It is dangerous to look straight at the Sun. When you play in the sunshine, always wear a hat, sunglasses and suncream.

dangerous – *not safe*

Fast Mercury

Mercury is a small planet that orbits very close to the Sun. The Sun's light makes Mercury's days incredibly hot, but nights on Mercury are bitterly cold – much colder than any freezer. This is because there is no air to stop the heat from escaping.

Rocks galore!

The surface of Mercury is dry and rocky with gigantic cliffs. Mercury also has huge craters (hollows) caused by the fall of rocks millions of years ago.

Mighty Mariner

The spacecraft
Mariner 10 flew past
Mercury three times
in 1974 and 1975.
It took photographs
of about half the planet.

God of speed

According to the myths of
ancient Rome, Mercury
was the messenger of the
gods. He was supposed
to fly quickly because he
had wings on his heels.

Roasting Venus

Venus is the closest planet to Earth. On Venus, the sky is yellow and cloudy. The clouds trap the Sun's heat, which makes Venus a very, very hot planet.

Violent volcanoes

There are massive volcanoes on Venus. Some are much higher than any mountains on Earth. Venus's most famous volcano is called Maat Mons. It is over nine kilometres high. Sometimes on Venus, all the volcanoes erupt together, covering the whole planet in lava.

lava – rock that is so hot, it has melted

Lightning strikes

The air on Venus is full of deadly acid, and lightning flickers in the sky. Many spaceships have visited Venus, but they have been destroyed by the heat and acid in the air.

acid – a substance that can eat away other substances

Our planet Earth

Earth is the planet that we live on. Most of its surface is covered with water, so from space, the Earth looks blue. Together, the water, air and warmth of the Sun make life on Earth possible.

Life on Earth

There are over 30 million different types of plants and animals on Earth. They live everywhere, from the deepest ocean to the top of the highest mountain.

dolphins

Restless planet

Compared to the other planets in the Solar System, Earth has many volcanoes and earthquakes. Deep underground, the Earth is so hot that the rock is molten. When a volcano erupts, the molten rock escapes onto the planet's surface.

molten – melted

Earth's Moon

The Moon is our closest neighbour in space. Just as the Earth orbits the Sun, the Moon goes around planet Earth. There is no life or weather on the Moon – no clouds, wind, rain or snow.

Hide and seek

The Moon takes a month to go around the Earth. It also takes a month to spin around. Because of this, we only ever see one side of the Moon from Earth. However, spaceships have travelled around the Moon so we know what the far side looks like.

weather – how hot, cold, windy, dry or rainy it is

full Moon   *gibbous Moon*   *last quarter*   *crescent Moon*

Changing Moon

As the Moon moves, different parts of it are lit by the Sun. This makes it look as if the Moon is changing shape. The different shapes are called phases.

Crusty craters

Most of the Moon's craters were made millions of years ago when huge chunks of rock crashed into it.

Moon visit

The Moon is the only other world people have visited. On the Moon, astronauts weigh one-sixth as much as at home.

Buzzing around

In 1969, Buzz Aldrin (born 1930) and Neil Armstrong (born 1930) were the first astronauts to land on the Moon. They stayed there for 21 hours before returning to Earth.

Lunar Rover

In 1971, an electric car called the *Lunar Rover* was used to explore the Moon. So far, 12 people have visited the Moon. The last voyage was in 1972.

Famous footprints

Because there is no rain or wind to disturb the dust on the Moon's surface, the footprints left by the astronauts in 1969 are still there.

Rusty Mars

Mars is red because it is rusty. There is a lot of iron in the soil, and the air on Mars has made it turn red – just like rusty iron on Earth.

Poles of ice

Like Earth, the poles (the top and bottom ends of the planet) of Mars are covered in ice. The ice becomes thicker in winter.

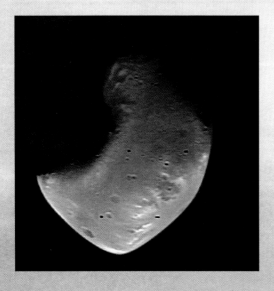

Two moons

Mars has two tiny moons called Phobos (left) and Deimos (above). Phobos is moving closer and closer to Mars, and scientists think that one day it will crash into Mars.

iron – *a metal, often used for making things*

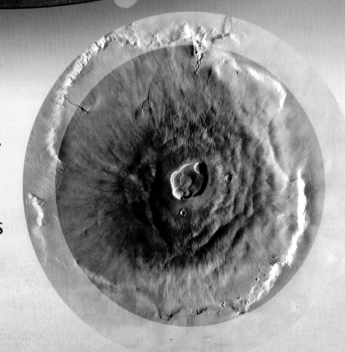

Mighty Mons

Mars's surface is covered with deserts, canyons, craters and gigantic dead volcanoes. Olympus Mons is the tallest volcano in the Solar System. It is 24 kilometres high.

canyons – deep, rocky valleys

Living with martians

Long ago, the air on Mars was thicker, and there were valleys filled with water. This means that there may have been life on the red planet.

Super Spirit

In 2004, *Spirit* landed on Mars after a seven-month journey through space. It sent pictures of Mars back to Earth, and studied the soil and rocks there.

probes – *spaceships that explore space but do not carry astronauts*

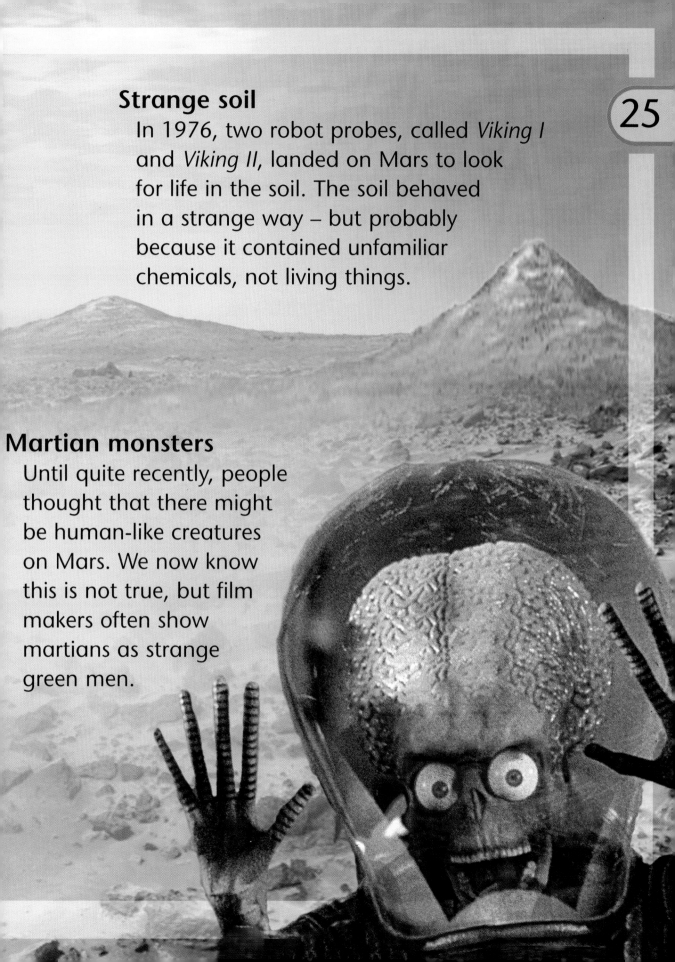

Strange soil

In 1976, two robot probes, called *Viking I* and *Viking II*, landed on Mars to look for life in the soil. The soil behaved in a strange way – but probably because it contained unfamiliar chemicals, not living things.

Martian monsters

Until quite recently, people thought that there might be human-like creatures on Mars. We now know this is not true, but film makers often show martians as strange green men.

Giant Jupiter

Jupiter is the biggest planet. It is 1,300 times the size of Earth. It spins around quickly, so its days are only ten hours long. Because it does not have a solid surface, it is impossible to land a spaceship on Jupiter.

Huge red spot
Jupiter is a very stormy planet. One storm has already lasted for over 300 years! From the Earth, this storm looks like a giant red spot.

Marvellous moons

Jupiter has many moons. The moon shown here, Io, has active volcanoes. Europa has an icy surface and Ganymede is the biggest moon in the Solar System – it is bigger than the planets Mercury and Pluto.

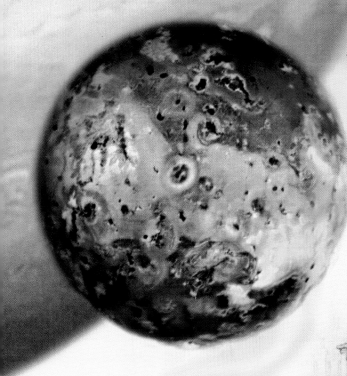

Great Galileo

In 1609, using a home-made telescope, the Italian scientist Galileo Galilei (1564–1642) discovered four of Jupiter's moons.

telescope – an invention that makes things look bigger

Ringed **Saturn**

Many people think that Saturn is the most beautiful world in the Solar System. Saturn is so light that if there were an ocean big enough, the planet would float in it.

Rings of rock

Saturn's rings are made of billions of pieces of rocks and dust. Although the planets Jupiter, Uranus and Neptune also have ring systems, theirs are not as bright or as big as Saturn's.

billion – *a thousand million*

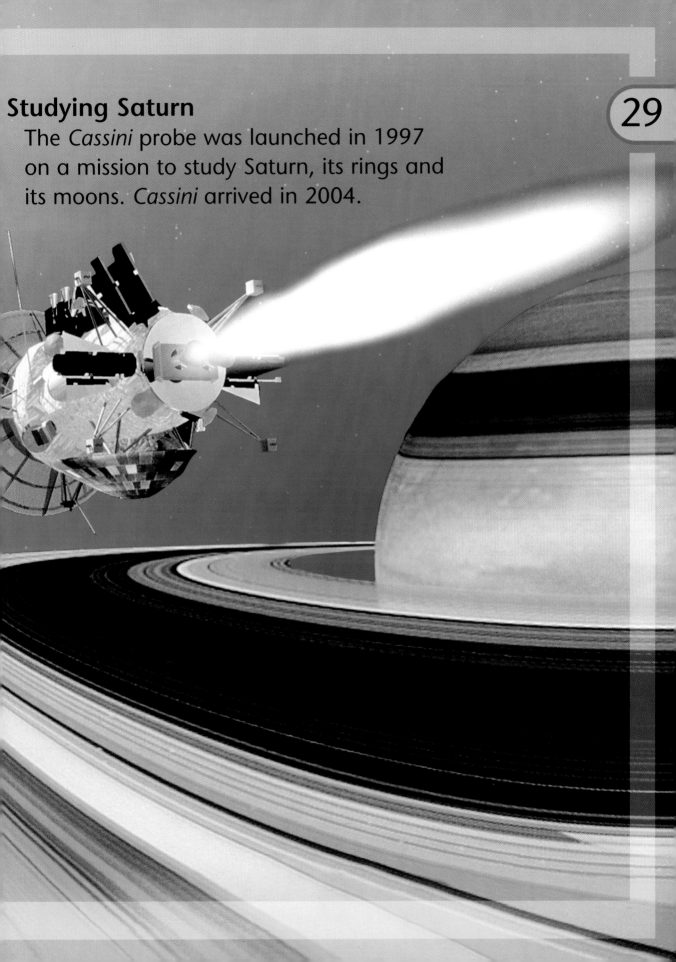

Studying Saturn

The *Cassini* probe was launched in 1997 on a mission to study Saturn, its rings and its moons. *Cassini* arrived in 2004.

Cold Uranus

Uranus is a huge, cold, blue-green world far out in space. It is surrounded by many black rings and icy moons. Because of the odd way it spins, nights on some parts of Uranus can last for more than 40 years.

Twisted Miranda

The surface of Miranda, one of Uranus's moons, is incredibly twisted and jumbled. It has cliffs over 20 kilometres high, enormous ridges, grooves and craters.

Uranus

groove – *a long thin line that is cut into a flat surface*

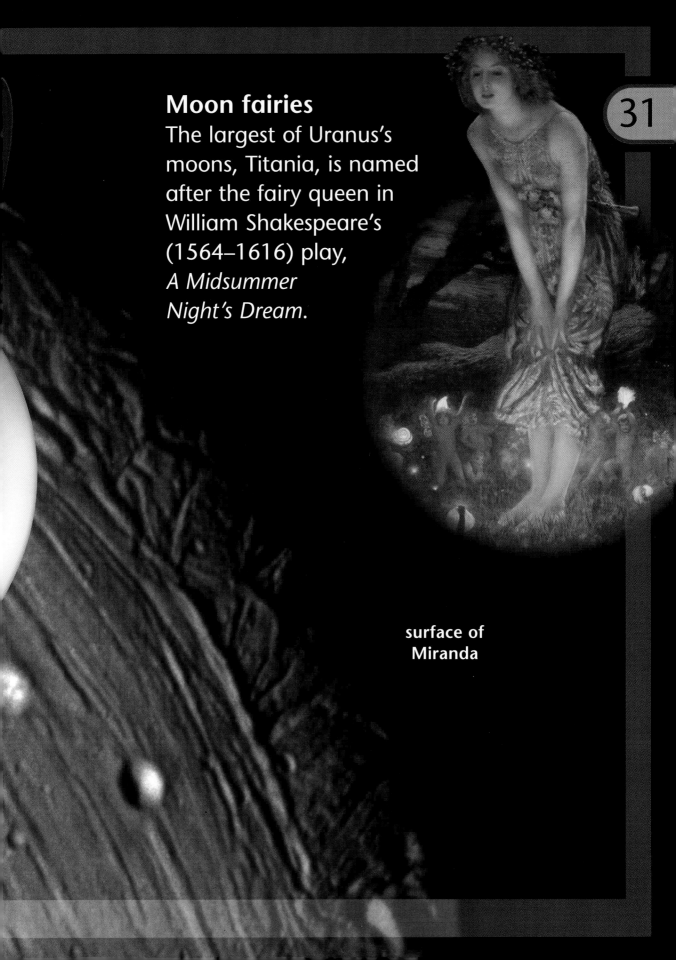

Moon fairies

The largest of Uranus's moons, Titania, is named after the fairy queen in William Shakespeare's (1564–1616) play, *A Midsummer Night's Dream.*

surface of
Miranda

32) Stormy Neptune

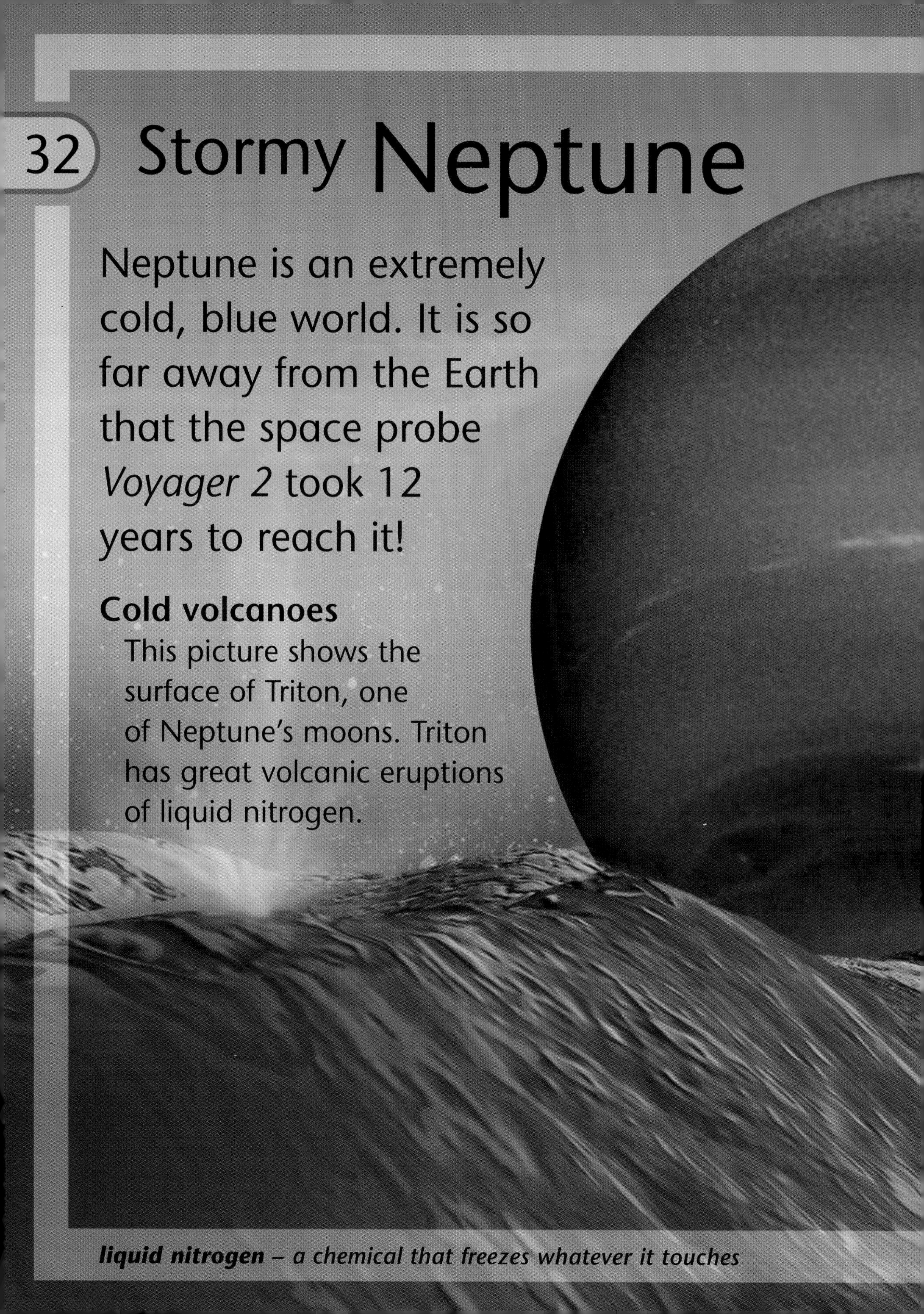

Neptune is an extremely cold, blue world. It is so far away from the Earth that the space probe *Voyager 2* took 12 years to reach it!

Cold volcanoes

This picture shows the surface of Triton, one of Neptune's moons. Triton has great volcanic eruptions of liquid nitrogen.

liquid nitrogen – *a chemical that freezes whatever it touches*

Stormy clouds

Neptune is the stormiest planet. The winds there can blow up to 2,000 kilometres per hour – three times as fast as Earth's hurricanes! Sometimes, storm clouds appear as white streaks or dark spots on its cloudy surface.

hurricane – a dangerous and violent storm

Distant Pluto

Pluto is the planet farthest from the Sun. It is tiny, reddish-brown and smaller than Earth's moon. Because it is so small and distant, Pluto can only be seen from Earth with a powerful telescope.

Colossal Charon

Pluto has an enormous
moon called Charon.
This giant was discovered
only in 1978. Charon
is darker and greyer
than Pluto but, like Pluto,
it is also covered in rocks
and ice.

In the dark

If you visited Pluto, the Sun
would look like a bright star.
Pluto is so far away from the
Sun that it is always dark. It is
the only planet that no spaceship
has reached, so we do not
really know what it looks like.

Failed planet

Beyond Mars and Jupiter there are billions of pieces of rock and metal called asteroids. They are much smaller than planets. Scientists believe that the asteroids are pieces of a planet that failed to form.

Asteroid belt

Most asteroids can be found in two regions or 'belts'. One of the belts is between Mars and Jupiter, and the other is beyond Neptune.

region – *area*

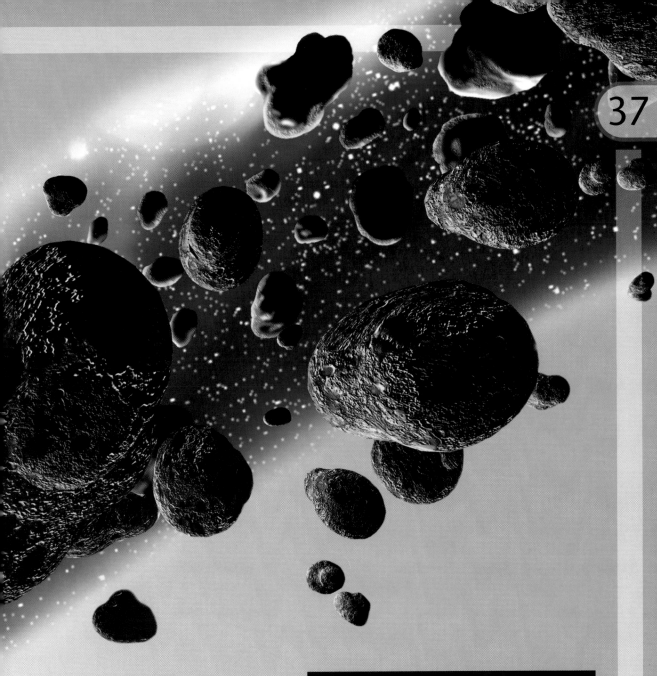

Asteroid Ida

Ida is a small, potato-shaped asteroid with its own tiny moon. In 1993 the *Galileo* space probe took pictures of Ida as it flew past.

Space
travellers

Comets are visitors from the
outer parts of the Solar System.
They are lumps of ice and dust: a bit
like dirty icebergs drifting through space.
When the comets are close to the Sun,
the ice turns to gas.

Return of the comet

All comets orbit the Sun.
Some take hundreds,
thousands or even
millions of years to
return. Halley's comet
returns only every 76
years. This famous
tapestry shows Halley's
comet (top left) in 1066.

Two-tailed Hale-Bopp

As a comet moves closer to the Sun, it forms two tails. One of the tails is made of gas and the other of dust. The gas tail points away from the Sun. In this picture of comet Hale-Bopp, the gas tail is blue and the dust tail is whitish.

Comet crash!

In 1994, pieces of a comet called Shoemaker-Levy 9 broke up and smashed into Jupiter. This left patches in Jupiter's atmosphere that lasted for many months.

Space rubble

There are many pieces of rock and dust drifting in space. These objects are called meteoroids. Many meteoroids are left behind by comets.

Shooting stars!

Every year, 200,000 tonnes of meteoroids fall through the Earth's atmosphere. As large meteoroids rush through the air, they become so hot that they glow. This falling glow is called a meteor or a shooting star.

tonne – 1,000 kilograms

Huge Hoba

Meteors that land on the Earth are called meteorites. The heaviest known meteorite is Hoba West. It was found in 1920 in Namibia and weighs about 60 tonnes – that is about as heavy as nine elephants!

Way out there

In 1961, a Russian called Yuri Gagarin (1934–1968) became the first person to journey into space and go right around the Earth. Since then, many astronauts have travelled through space.

Drifting through space

Exploring space is dangerous. Sometimes, astronauts leave their spaceships to 'walk' in space. This astronaut is wearing a device that can push him back to his spaceship if he starts to drift away.

Life in space

In space there is no air, nothing has any weight and there is no 'up' or 'down', which can make life difficult. Some space travellers get space-sick, just like people on Earth get sea-sick.

Bedroom planetarium

Dome-shaped buildings called planetariums have lights that show the night sky. Use a torch to make your own starry sky.

You will need
- Torch
- Pencil
- Card and sheet of paper
- Pair of scissors
- Sticky tape

1 Place the torch on the sheet of card so that you can draw around the front side of it. Using the pencil, draw carefully around the torch.

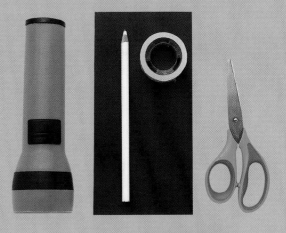

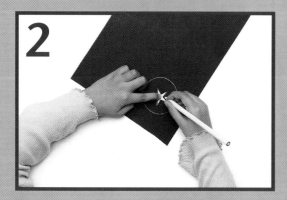

2 To make a star-shaped stencil, draw a star on paper and cut it out. Place the stencil in the torch-shape and draw around it.

3 Using the pair of scissors, carefully cut out both shapes. You should now be left with card that has a star shape in the middle.

4

Use sticky tape to fix the card to the front of the torch. Switch off all the lights and shine the torch to create a fabulously starry sky. For something different, try cutting out a shape of the Moon.

Watch the Moon

Find the craters!

Not only are there craters on the surface of the Moon, but over a month, our nearest neighbour also changes shape. On a clear night, use binoculars to look for the Moon's craters. Never look at the Sun with binoculars as this will damage your eyes.

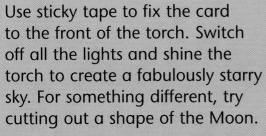

Whenever you see the Moon, whether at night or during the day, draw its shape on the correct date in a calendar. After a few months, your calendar will show you how the Moon goes through a series of changes (called phases).

Crazy comets

Finding new comets

New comets are discovered every year, but most of them are too faint to see without binoculars or a telescope.

1

To make big bits of space dust, place two digestive biscuits on a plate. Using the wooden spoon, crush the biscuits into large pieces.

You will need
- 2 large dinner plates
- Digestive biscuits
- Wooden spoon
- Hundreds and thousands
- Teaspoon
- Chocolate sprinkles
- Ice-cream scoop
- Chocolate ice-cream
- Ice-cream cone

2

To make smaller bits of space dust, add a large handful of hundreds and thousands to the crushed biscuits.

3

For extra space dirt, add two handfuls of chocolate sprinkles to the mixture. Use a teaspoon to give the space dust a good stir.

4

For the comet's head, use an ice-cream scoop to make a ball of ice-cream. Cover the ball of ice-cream in the dust mixture.

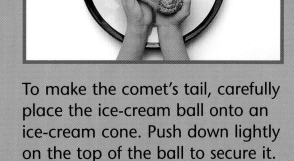

6

To make the comet's tail, carefully place the ice-cream ball onto an ice-cream cone. Push down lightly on the top of the ball to secure it.

5

Roll the ice-cream back into a ball-shape. If the ice-cream has started to melt, put it on another plate in the freezer.

Although you would never be able to eat a real comet, such as Hale-Bopp, this one is made from delicious ice-cream, so it tastes great!

Index